E is for Evergreen

A Washington Alphabet

Written by Marie and Roland Smith
Illustrated by Linda Holt Ayriss

The authors would like to give a special thank you to Mary Palmer and Amy Twito at the Seattle Public Library.

For the letter J: Photo reference courtesy of University of Washington Libraries, Special Collections Division. Negative No. UW 23527z

For the letter L: Photo reference of Bertha Landes courtesy of Scott Kline and the city of Seattle.

For the letter U: Special thanks to William Galvani, director of the Naval Undersea Museum. Also, special thanks to Officer Mike Kolodner.

Credit for observatory photo reference: Stephen R. Stout, Goldendale Observatory.

Sleeping Bear Press
310 North Main Street, Suite 300
Chelsea, MI 48118
www.sleepingbearpress.com

Printed and bound in Canada.

10 9 8 7 6 5 4 3 2 1

Library of Congress Cataloging-in-Publication Data

Smith, Marie, 1951-
E is for evergreen : a Washington alphabet / written by Marie Smith and Roland Smith ; illustrated by Linda Holt Ayriss.
p. cm.
ISBN 1-58536-143-7
1. Washington (State)—Juvenile literature. 2. English language—Alphabet—Juvenile literature. I. Smith, Roland, 1951- II. Ayriss, Linda. III. Title.
F891.3.S65 2004
979.7—dc22   2004005260

To Jack Charles Glaze.
We will love you all of our days.

AHNA AND GRAMPS

❧

To Dave, Erin, and my mom for all their help and support.

LINDA

A is for Apple.
So many on a tree—
crisp and ripe, ready to pick.
Plenty for you and me!

Washington is the nation's top apple-producing state. The apple was selected as the state fruit in 1989, and is the most recognized symbol of Washington world-wide. Americans eat about 20 pounds of fresh apples a year—six out of ten are Washington apples. Washington grows nine varieties of apples to sell. The apple season starts in August and ends in November. During a season workers handpick over three billion apples for markets all over the world.

Eating crisp, juicy, Washington apples year-round is possible due to a process called controlled atmosphere storage. Apples are stored in specially designed buildings to control the temperature, oxygen, carbon dioxide, and humidity, which slows the ripening process. Timing of harvest is critical for good storage results. Apples picked too soon or too ripe do not store well—they have to be just right! Apples are given grades—Washington Extra Fancy apples are the very best.

A a

Bigfoot is a cryptid—a cryptid is an animal that is believed to exist, but hasn't been proven to exist scientifically. Cryptozoology is the study of cryptids. Encounters with Bigfoot in the Pacific Northwest have been going on for hundreds of years. Long ago Native Americans called them Sasquatch. Dozens of Bigfoot sightings have been reported around Mount St. Helens. People describing this shy creature say it's up to 11 feet tall and weighs up to 2,500 pounds. Apelike with a broad, flattened nose and a lipless mouth, it does not speak but emits a roaring scream.

B is also for the Boeing Company. William E. Boeing lived in Seattle. After attending the first U.S. air races in Los Angeles, he became fascinated with flight and airplanes. His interest would eventually lead to the beginning of the Boeing Company. Boeing is the world's largest manufacturer of commercial airplanes and spacecraft and it is the Seattle area's largest employer.

B is for Bigfoot.
People wonder to this day,
  are they fact or fiction?
It's difficult to say.

While sailing around the world in 1792, Captain Robert Gray found the Columbia River and named it after his ship, *Columbia Rediviva*. Starting at the base of the Canadian Rockies, the river flows down and across Washington for more than 1,200 miles before joining the Pacific Ocean. It has 10 major tributaries. (A tributary is water that flows into a larger body of water.) Its most important tributary is the Snake River. The Columbia is the largest river in the western United States.

C is also for the Columbian mammoth, Washington's state fossil since 1998. About two million years ago the first North American mammoths migrated across the Bering Strait from Asia down through Alaska. The mammoths became extinct about 10,000 years ago. Fossils of the Columbian mammoth have been discovered on the Olympic Peninsula.

C is for Columbia River,
through our state it flows.
Other rivers adding to it,
along the way it grows.

Washington has a dragon.
It's tiny but it can fly.
Dragonfly starts with D.
How many can you spy?

The Green Darner Dragonfly became t[...]
official state insect in 1997 after stude[...]
at Crestwood Elementary in Kent brou[...]
the idea of a state insect to the legislat[...]
Children all over the state voted and [...]
Green Darner Dragonfly won.

Dragonflies, like the dragons of legend[...]
have powerful heads with large jaws, a[...]
very long tails. Although its wingspan [...]
only four to six inches, it can fly 25 t[...]
35 miles per hour. The Washington Sta[...]
dragonfly is easy to recognize by its bri[...]
green color. Some people are afraid [...]
dragonflies, but they are harmless. Luc[...]
for us, one of its favorite foods is the[...]
mosquito—earning the nickname
"mosquito hawk."

E is for the Evergreen State,
forests of old growth and rain.
Our nickname comes from
nature's unbroken chain.

Washington was nicknamed the Evergreen State because of its abundant forests. Some are old growth forests that have been undisturbed by humans for centuries and have a multilevel canopy. Ancient trees tower over younger shade-tolerant trees. Downed logs and standing dead trees, called snags, provide homes for dozens of birds, mammals, and insects. The snags slowly decompose and return nutrients to the soil.

Washington also has temperate rain forests with huge Sitka spruce, western hemlock, Douglas fir, and western red cedar trees all at the top. Then come bigleaf maples, black cottonwoods, and red alder. At the bottom are vine maple with many ferns and mosses that give the ground a soft cover. Up to 200 inches of rain a year keep these rain forests green. The word "temperate" describes the temperatures as moderate, neither hot nor cold.

The Olympic National Forest has temperate rain forests and old growth forests. Some parts of these forests are both temperate rain forest *and* old growth combined—but not always!

Ee

Originally Washington was part of the Oregon Territory, then it became the Washington Territory, and finally America's 42nd state on November 11, 1889. Washington is the only state named after a president, has the only state flag with a picture of a president, and has the only state flag that is green.

F is for fish. The steelhead trout, Washington's state fish, has a silver-gray spotted back and a white belly with a stripe of opalescent pink down the middle.

Flower also starts with **f**. In 1892, even though women were not allowed to vote, voting booths were set up and women throughout the state cast their vote for the state flower. When the ballots were counted the coast rhododendron won over clover. The rhododendron can be pink, yellow, white, red, or purple in color.

Finally! **F** is for Father's Day, started in 1910 by Sonora Louise Smart Dodd from Spokane to honor her father, a Civil War veteran.

F is for our state Flag,
with the face of a president,
even though George Washington
never was a resident!

G is for Goldendale Observatory.
This is a place to gaze
at all the stars and planets,
a place that will amaze.

Goldendale Observatory State Park g[...]
its start from four amateur astronome[...]
who built a 24-inch, Cassegrain reflecti[...]
telescope and wanted a home for it.
(A Cassegrain telescope is a wide-ang[...]
reflecting telescope that uses two m[...]
rors.) They donated the telescope to t[...]
town of Goldendale. The town built t[...]
observatory on top of a 2,100-foot-hi[...]
hill. It is one of the nation's largest
public telescopes and can be used b[...]
anyone who wants to gaze at the sta[...]
and planets.

G is also for gem. Washington's state g[...]
is petrified wood, adopted in 1975. Lo[...]
ago parts of Washington were swam[...]
with many cypress, oak, elm, and gink[...]
trees. Volcanic eruptions covered the[...]
trees with lava. After a long time, wa[...]
seeped into the wood, replacing it w[...]
silica, which petrified many logs. Petrif[...]
wood is perfect in form and detail to t[...]
original wood. The Ginkgo Petrified For[...]
State Park in Vantage is a registered[...]
national natural landmark.

H is for Horses,
a Native American breed.
Appaloosa came from the Palouse Hills
known for their beauty, grace, and speed.

The Palouse and Nez Perce tribes lived in the area that eventually became Washington, Oregon, and Idaho. Known for their great horsemanship, they were thought to be the first tribes to breed horses for specific traits. Their beautiful spotted horses were known for their endurance, intelligence, speed, and gentle nature. The horses were originally called Palouse horses, named after the Palouse River, but later it was changed to the Appaloosa.

H is also for Hanford. In 1943 during World War II our government moved residents out of the southeastern part of Washington. Because of wartime security no one was told why. This area became the Hanford Nuclear Reservation. Hanford was built to secretly make plutonium, one of the main ingredients in an atomic bomb. The first atomic explosion in July 1945 at Alamogordo, New Mexico and the bomb that was dropped on Nagasaki, Japan, August 9, 1945 both used plutonium from Hanford.

H h

The water between Washington and Canada is made up of the Strait of Juan de Fuca, the Strait of Georgia, the Hood Canal, and Puget Sound. Whidbey Island, the largest island in this area, measures 45 miles in length. The San Juan Islands are located in the northern reaches of Puget Sound. There are about 175 islands in this group. Washington has the largest ferry system in the United States to move travelers between the islands and the mainland.

According to American folklore, Paul Bunyan was a giant lumberjack with a pet blue ox named Babe. He was famous for his great strength. He dug out Puget Sound to float huge logs to mills and started the logging business in the Pacific Northwest.

Puget Sound is named after Lieutenant Peter Puget who surveyed the lower part of the sound in May 1792.

I is for Islands.
Bainbridge and Cypress are two.
San Juan, Lopez, Whidbey,
Orcas—can you name a few?

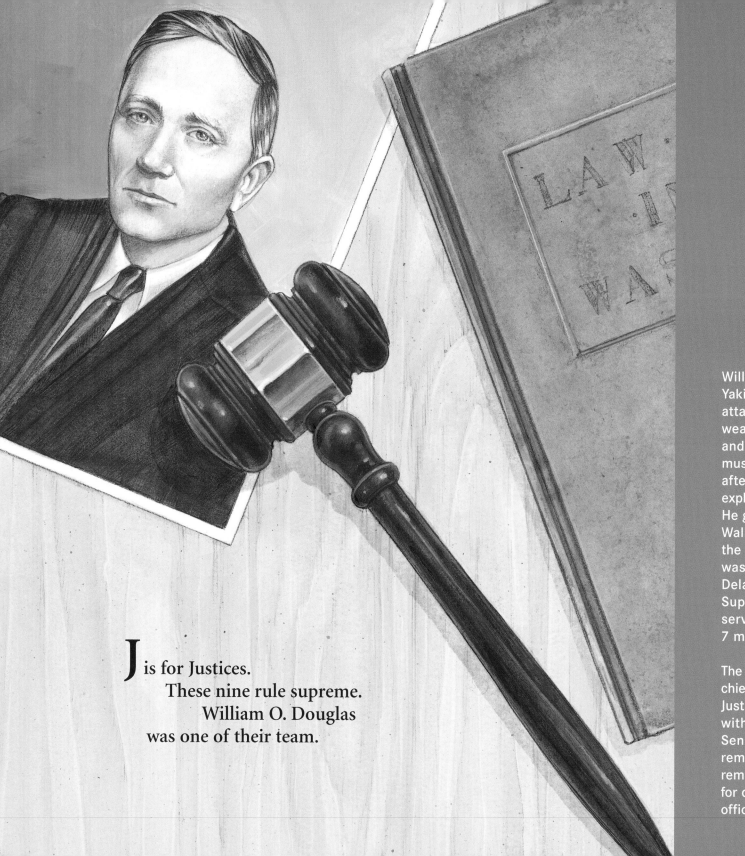

Jj

J is for Justices.
These nine rule supreme.
William O. Douglas
was one of their team.

William Orville Douglas grew up in Yakima. At an early age he survived an attack of polio that left him physically weak. He vowed to improve his mind and worked hard to strengthen his muscles. He came to love the outdoors after spending many hours hiking and exploring the mountains of Washington. He graduated from Whitman College in Walla Walla and wrote many books on the Pacific Northwest. William Douglas was appointed by President Franklin Delano Roosevelt as a Justice of the Supreme Court on April 17, 1939 and served on the court for 36 years and 7 months, the longest term ever.

The Supreme Court has nine members—a chief justice and eight associate justices. Justices are appointed by the president with the advice and consent of the Senate. Once appointed, justices may remain in office for life. Congress can remove a justice through impeachment for corrupt behavior or other abuses of office, but has never done so.

K is for Kites.
　　See thousands at Long Beach.
Children run and chase
　　　as they fly out of reach.

Every year Long Beach holds an International Kite Festival which is the largest kite festival in the Western Hemisphere. It is held on the Long Beach Peninsula which has 28 miles of continuous beach. About 150,000 people come to fly their kites or just watch. The kites are made of different materials and come in all sizes, shapes, and colors. Teams and individuals compete, hoping to set world records—like the biggest kite, the longest flight time for a kite, or the number of kites flown at one time.

The first known kites came from China more than 2,000 years ago. For centuries kites have been used for scientific research, weather observation, even espionage. One of the most famous uses of a kite was Benjamin Franklin's experiment with lightning. The Wright brothers used box kites to test their ideas before making the first airplane in 1903.

Kites were named after a graceful, soaring bird called a *kite*.

VOTE FOR LANDES

L is for Landes—
it never had been done—
Seattle chose a lady mayor,
the country's number one.

Bertha Knight Landes was elected mayor of Seattle in 1926 and was the first woman to lead a major American c A wife and mother of three, she ran o platform of "municipal housekeeping vowing to clean up city government. S offered one dollar a year to anyone w would pledge to report reckless drivi Her single term ended in 1928, but s remained a civic leader and role mod for women.

L is for ladies. Dixy Lee Ray, born in Tacoma, became the first female gove nor of Washington in November 197 Patty Murray, born in Bothell, becam Washington's first female senator in 199 On November 8, 1910, the Washingt state legislature granted women the rig to vote, becoming the fifth state in t nation to do so. Women in many oth states had to wait until 1920 after the ratification of the 19th Amendment t the United States Constitution givin all women the right to vote.

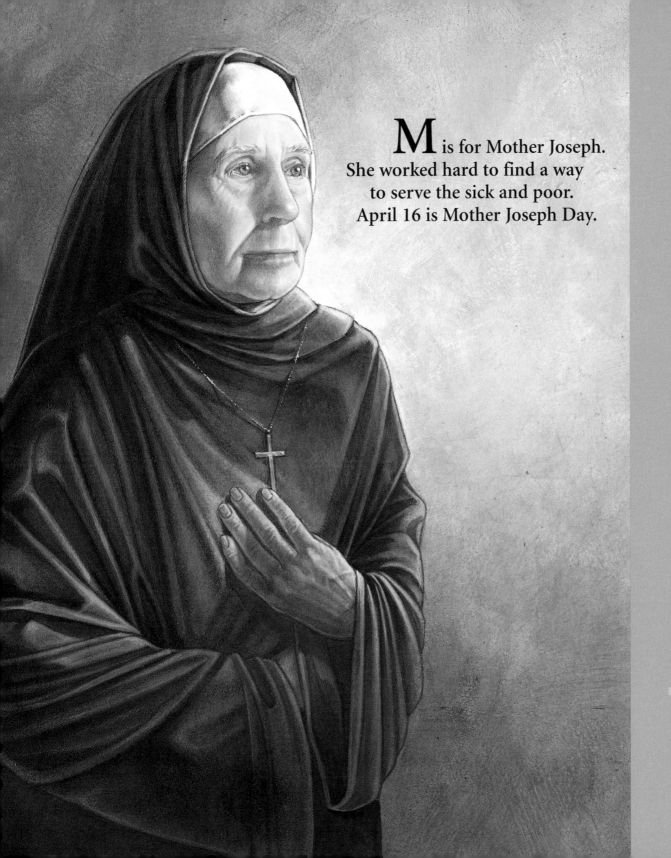

M is for Mother Joseph.
She worked hard to find a way
to serve the sick and poor.
April 16 is Mother Joseph Day.

Mother Joseph and four other Sisters of Providence arrived at Fort Vancouver in 1856 to begin a mission caring for the sick, old, and poor. Mother Joseph built eleven hospitals, seven academies, five Indian schools, and two orphanages. Students from Vancouver brought attention to her work before the state legislature. April 16, 1999 was chosen as a day to "recognize and honor Mother Joseph on the occasion of the 176th year of her birth." Mother Joseph also represents Washington in the National Statuary Hall in Washington D.C. along with Marcus Whitman.

Marcus Whitman established the Waiilatpu Mission in 1836. Narcissa, his wife, was one of the first white women in the Oregon Territory.

M is also for Microsoft. In 1975, Bill Gates and Paul Allen from Seattle founded Microsoft, which revolutionized the world with software used to make computers work better.

M
m

N n

On July 17, 1897, the steamboat *Portland* sailed into Seattle harbor with two tons of gold and news of a gold strike. Gold was found on the small Klondike River which joins the Yukon River at Dawson City, Canada. From 1897 to 1898, tens of thousands of people from around the world stopped in Seattle to purchase food, clothing, equipment, pack animals, and steamship tickets for the trip north. The merchants that provided the goods and services ended up with more gold than most miners.

The Klondike Gold Rush National Historical Park, located in downtown Seattle, honors the state's starting point for the miners going to the Yukon goldfields.

N is for Nordstrom. John Nordstrom was one of the miners on the Klondike. He came back with gold and started a shoe store with Carl Wallin. Today Nordstrom is a fun place to shop for more than just shoes!

N is for the Nuggets
at the end of the Yukon trail.
A lucky few found gold
but thousands went and failed

Olympia is Washington's capital city. It is on the southern tip of Puget Sound with a view of the Olympic Mountains across the water to the north and Mt. Rainier to the east. Explorers and fur traders traveled to the Puget Sound area in the early 1800s. Back then it was home to Native Americans whose villages had occupied the site for thousands of years. They called it "The Black Bear Place."

George Washington Bush was the leader of the first settlers to the Puget Sound area and was the first African American to settle in the territory. He brought his family west by wagon train in 1844. Besides taking care of their own five sons, George and his wife, Isabel, helped children who became orphaned while on the trip west. He settled near Olympia in an area called Bush Prairie.

O is for Olympia
    on the shores of Puget Sound.
Here our state government
    and capital can be found.

P is for the Peace Arch,
on our border it stands,
a symbol of the unity
between two common lands.

The Peace Arch is located in Blaine, Washington and White Rock, British Columbia. The arch was built to honor a century of peace between America and Canada. This border is the longest undefended border in the world. The words "May These Gates Never Be Closed" is written on the bronze gates that are always open. Also written on the U.S. side of the arch is "Children of a Common Mother." Written on the Canadian side is "Brethren Dwelling Together in Unity."

Sam Hill first had the idea to build the peace arch. He devoted his life to business, civic affairs, philanthropy, and good roads. He built Marysville Museum and the Stonehenge replica which is the first monument in our nation to honor those who died during World War I. Both overlook the Columbia River.

P is also for the Pacific Ocean. It is the western border of Washington State. Washington has 150 miles of coastline.

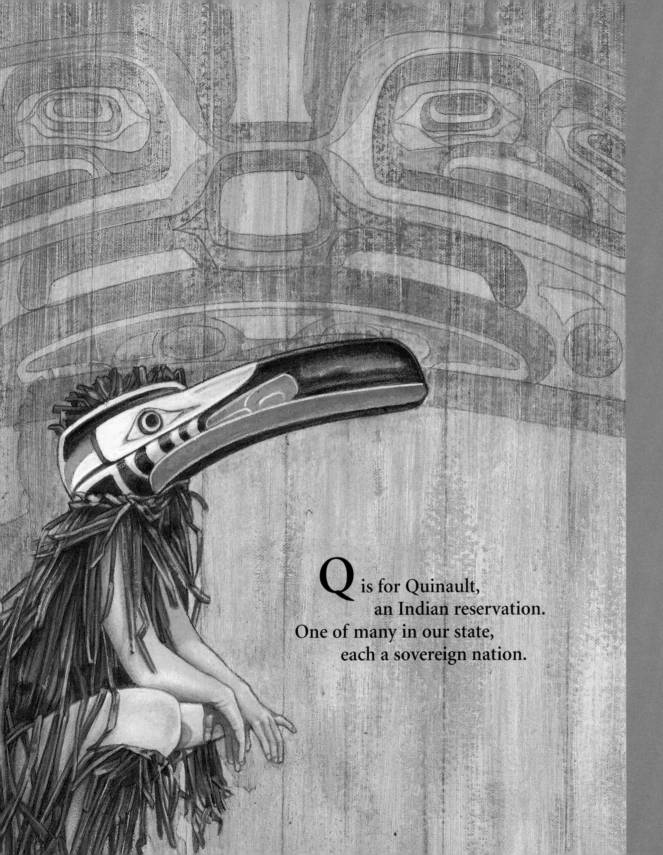

Thousands of years ago Native Americans named the Queets, Quileutes, Hohs, and Makahs lived north of the Quinault River. To the south of the river lived the Copalis, Humptulips, Wishkah, Chinook, and Chehalis tribes. When the Native Americans moved onto the Quinault Reservation they all were considered members of the Quinault tribe. The Quinault Indian Nation established an elective government ruled by a Tribal Council in 1922.

There are eight Indian reservations in Washington. Reservations are lands that are recognized by the federal government as separate sovereign nations. Native American tribes are able to control the land, natural resources, and education within reservation boundaries and create their own laws.

Q is for Quinault,
an Indian reservation.
One of many in our state,
each a sovereign nation.

R is for Rainier,
Washington's highest peak.
Mountaineers climb its slopes
for adventure that they seek.

Mount Rainier is 14,410 feet high. It is Washington's highest peak. Before 1792 when British Captain George Vancouver first saw the mountain and named it for his friend, Rear Admiral Peter Rainier, Native Americans called it Tahoma. The first documented climb to the summit of Mount Rainier was in 1870 by Hazard Stevens and Philemon Van Trump. Since then it has become a popular mountain for climbers. In 1890 Yelm schoolteacher Fay Fuller became the first woman documented to climb the mountain. Mount Rainier was declared a national park in 1899. The Wonderland Trail is a 93-mile loop around the mountain that takes about 10 days to walk.

R is also for Roosevelt Elk. These elk are originally from Washington. They are named after President Theodore Roosevelt.

Rr

The Space Needle sits in an area called Seattle Center. The 605-foot structure was built for the 1962 Seattle World's Fair to symbolize our future in space. It is the most recognized symbol of Seattle. An observation deck circles the top and allows a 360-degree view of the city. At night the stars and moon make a beautiful backdrop. On a clear day, views of Mount Rainier, the Olympic Mountains, Mount Baker, Lake Union, Lake Washington, and Elliott Bay can be seen. All the trees and green of the water confirm Seattle's nickname as the *Emerald City.*

Seattle is Washington's biggest city and is the only major city in America named after a Native American. Seattle is named after Chief Seattle (also spelled *Seatlh* or *Sealth*), a Salish Indian who befriended the first settlers. Chief Seattle was known for his peaceful and helpful ways.

Seattle and Space Needle start with the letter S
Travel 605 feet to the top for a view that will impr

S s

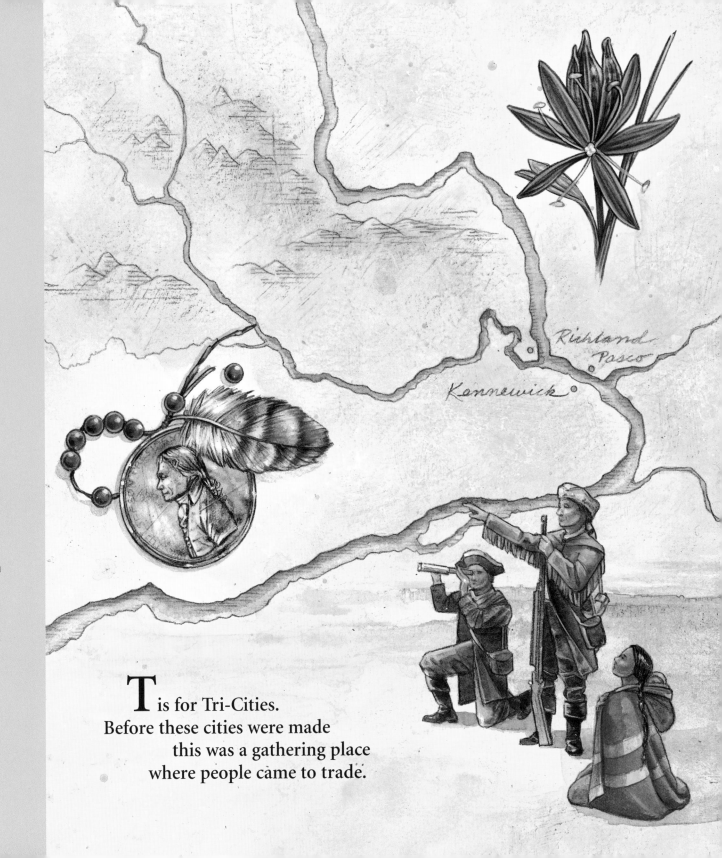

asco, Kennewick, and Richland are
nown as the tri-cities. This is the fourth
argest populated area in Washington.

he Lewis and Clark expedition
amped in the tri-cities area in October
f 1805. The expedition made detailed
escriptions of plant and animal life and
ocumented the Columbia River and its
ibutaries. This area was an important
athering place for trade among the
alouse, Walla Walla, Wanapum, Yakama
nd Umatilla Indians. With Toussaint
harbonneau and Sacajawea as their
nterpreters, Lewis and Clark met with
e local tribes and gave them Jefferson
edals as a symbol of peace. The
xpedition stopped here again on
heir return in 1806.

he Hanford Reach in Richland is the
ast free-flowing stretch of the Columbia
iver located within Washington and
emains unchanged since Lewis and
lark explored it. In June 2000 it
ecame a national monument.

T is for Tri-Cities.
Before these cities were made
this was a gathering place
where people came to trade.

U is for the U.S. Navy,
   Their ships come and go—
      carriers on the surface,
   submarines down below.

Navy facilities and property total more than 28,000 acres of land in Washington. Naval Station Everett is home to three destroyers, three frigates, and one nuclear-powered aircraft carrier. Naval Submarine Base Bangor is homeport for the Trident nuclear submarines. Whidbey Island Naval Air Station was built as a base for seaplane patrol operations and is also the center for search and rescue crews.

Puget Sound Naval Shipyard in Bremerton, founded in 1891, is the largest shipyard on the West Coast. It is also homeport for a nuclear aircraft carrier, two nuclear cruisers, and three fleet support ships. Part of Puget Sound Naval Base is a national historic landmark.

Washington recognizes all branches of the armed services with one of the largest Armed Forces Day parades in the country. Every year tens of thousands of people attend the Bremerton's Armed Forces Day parade which is one of only seven events in the country officially recognized by the Department of Defense.

U
u

On May 18, 1980, Mount St. Helens erupted with a force of 21,000 atomic bombs and leveled over 200 square miles of forest. It killed 60 people, thousands of animals, and hundreds of thousands of birds and fish. Mount St. Helens became a National Volcanic Monument in 1983.

Washington has five major volcanoes— Mount Baker, Glacier Peak, Mount Rainier, Mount Adams, and Mount St. Helens. These volcanoes are part of the Cascade Range, a volcanic group of mountains that stretch from south-western British Columbia to northern California. Each of these volcanoes, except Mount Adams, have erupted within the last 250 years. Volcanoes do not erupt at regular intervals, and no one knows when they will erupt next.

V v

V is for Volcanoes—
    Mount St. Helens and her blast,
what a big disaster.
    We hope it was her last!

W is for Western hemlock.
Here birds sing and hop.
See the tiny goldfinch
right up near the top.

The Willow Goldfinch (or American Goldfinch as it is also called) became Washington's state bird in 1951. Known for its pretty song, it is a delicate bird about 5 inches tall. The male has a yellow body with a black tail and a patch of black on its head. The wings are black with a white stripe. In the winter the feathers turn olive brown with a little yellow. The female stays olive-brown with a black tail and black wings with a white stripe. Every spring the female lays four to six bluish-white eggs. The male's job is to bring food to the female while she sits on her eggs. He continues his work for the chicks after they hatch.

In 1947, the western hemlock (Tsuga heterophylla) became the Washington state tree. Washington offers the hemlock a perfect place to grow—cool moist areas with lots of shade. Western hemlock is a tall, straight, and beautiful evergreen tree with numerous delicate fan-like leaves.

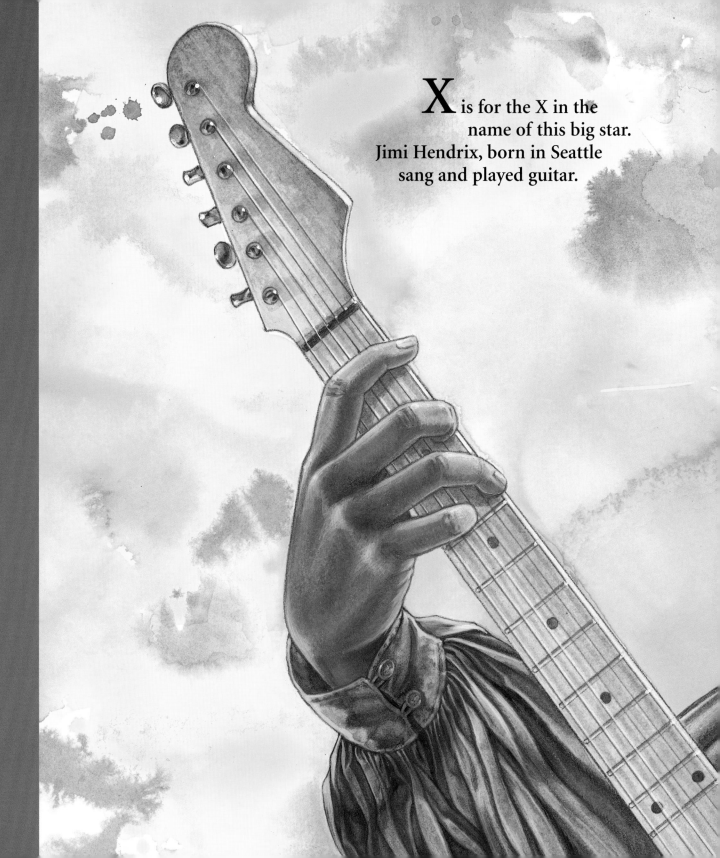

mi Hendrix was born on November 5, 1942 in Seattle. He was 11 years old when he was given his first guitar. He had an ear for music and as a teenager aught himself to play guitar by listening o records by blues guitarists like B.B. ing, Muddy Waters, Chuck Berry, and ddie Cochran. In high school he played with a band called The Rocking Kings. He later formed his own band called The mi Hendrix Experience. In 1968 he was amed artist of the year by *Billboard* nd *Rolling Stone* magazines. He is still onsidered one of the world's greatest uitarists that ever lived. He recorded ve albums, which later impacted count- ess other musicians, before he died n 1970 at age 27.

xperience Music Project, located Seattle Center, was built by Paul llen, co-founder of Microsoft. EMP is music museum that tells the story of opular music in America. The Hendrix allery of the museum tells the story f Jimi Hendrix.

X

X

X is for the X in the
name of this big star.
Jimi Hendrix, born in Seattle
sang and played guitar.

Y is for the Yakima Valley
where sun and irrigation
help produce fruit and vegetables
that feed our entire nation.

In 1852 missionaries Charles Pandosy and Louis d'Herbomez, along with Yakama tribes people, dug the first irrigation ditch in the Yakima Valley. The ditch was filled with water from Ahtanum Creek. Irrigation eventually changed the natural sagebrush desert into a valley known as the fruit bowl of the nation. The Yakima Valley is the largest producer of Washington apples. Peaches and cherries, along with many other fruits and vegetables, are also grown here. This valley has 300 days of sunshine and only eight inches of rain a year. The Yakima River is the largest source of water in this area. It starts in the Snoqualmie Pass, traveling through the valley until it meets the Columbia River.

Y is also for the golden yellow color of the wheat fields during harvest time. Approximately 2.4 million acres of wheat are planted in Washington. The color and beauty of the wheat at harvest time makes it one of the most photographed images of Washington.

Z is for Zoos.
Our state has three.
Animals from around the world
for everyone to see.

Woodland Park Zoo in northern Seattle was originally built as a home for Guy C. Phinney in 1887. His 180-acre estate on Green Lake had formal gardens with a menagerie of animals. He allowed the public to visit his beautiful gardens and enjoy the lake. After Mr. Phinney died, the city council voted to purchase the land to start a zoo. The zoo became the first zoo to show animals in naturalistic settings. Woodland Park Zoo now has over 300 animal species.

Point Defiance Zoo and Aquarium was founded in 1905 on 29 acres near the Puget Sound. Today it is a leader in captive breeding and reintroduction efforts for the endangered red wolf, and the zoo also participates in species survival plans for the endangered Bali mynah, golden lion tamarin, snow leopard, clouded leopard, radiated tortoise, and Asian elephant.

Northwest Trek is a 600-acre home to 200 North American animals. It is located south of Tacoma. It got its start from Dr. David and Connie Hellyer who gave 500 acres of land to Tacoma. Their dream was to create a park that would show North American wildlife in a natural setting. The park opened on July 17, 1975.

Zz

A Forest Full of Facts

1. What is the most recognized symbol of Washington State?

2. What is Washington's cryptid?

3. What is a Mosquito Hawk?

4. Who started Father's Day?

5. What is the largest island next to Washington?

6. Who was the first woman mayor of Seattle?

7. How long is Washington's coastline?

8. When was the last time Mount St. Helens erupted?

9. What was the band Jimi Hendrix played in during high school?

10. Where did Mt. Rainier get its name?

11. How long is the Wonderland Trail?

12. How tall is the space needle?

13. Where did the Lewis and Clark expedition camp in Washington?

14. Where is the largest producer of apples in Washington?

15. Who was the first African American to settle in Washington?

1. The apple
2. Bigfoot
3. A dragonfly
4. Sonora Louise Smart Dodd
5. Whidbey Island
6. Bertha Knight Landes
7. 150 miles
8. May 18, 1980
9. The Rocking Kings
10. British Captain George Vancouver named it after his friend Admiral Peter Rainier
11. 93 miles
12. 605 feet
13. In the Tri-Cities area
14. The Yakima Valley
15. George Washington Bush

Marie and Roland Smith

Marie and Roland grew up in Oregon and live on a small farm south of Portland. Roland is the author of many award-winning books for children including *Thunder Cave, Sasquatch, Jaguar, Zach's Lie,* and *The Captain's Dog: My Journey with the Lewis and Clark Tribe,* which won the Pacific Northwest Bookseller's Award. Marie and Roland also collaborated on *B is for Beaver: An Oregon Alphabet* published in 2003.

Linda Holt Ayriss

Illustrator Linda Holt Ayriss has managed to tame the evergreen forest surrounding her home on Bainbridge Island into beautiful natural gardens which provide her with endless inspiration. She uses acrylics and colored pencil to achieve the realism, sensitivity, and mood of her paintings. The island is a short ferry trip across Puget Sound from Seattle.

She has received a Society of Illustration Best of the West silver medal, and has appeared in the *Communication Arts Annual.* She has been drawing all of her life, but started illustrating as a professional in 1983.

She graduated from The Art Center College of Design in California and also holds a BFA from Pacific Lutheran University.